EDITED BY PATRICK WALSH

Patrick Walsh was born and lives in Dublin. He got into acting late in life, but has made up for lost time by being involved in three films and numerous stage productions, including playing the part of Jack in 'The Importance of Being Earnest'.

He produced snippets of Irish Theatre and is at present 'resting between projects', or as Oscar Wilde may have said, he is hard at work being idle. He studied in the Gaiety School of Acting and claims to prefer acting as it is so much more real than life.

Patrick is also available as a lecturer on themes and talks connected with Oscar Wilde.

"He can present a well-paced witty, knowledgeable and light-hearted quality lecture delivered in a relaxed and informal manner."

Carmen Cullen, Director
The Oscar Wilde Autumn School,
For further information contact Patrick on 01 8404284
Overseas Call 003531-8404284
Website coming soon: www.oscarwildefanclub.com

This Book is Dedicated to
Tim and George Walsh
and warmest thanks to the kind advice
from Merlin Holland,
Grandson of Oscar Wilde

WHAT PEOPLE SAID ABOUT OSCAR WILDE

Nelson Mandella
What kept his spirits up in prison was the Oscar Wilde quotation
We are all in the gutter but some of us are looking at the stars.

John Lennon of Beatle fame
He was the master of rebellion.

Winston churchill
The one person i am looking forward to meeting in the afterlife is
Oscar Wilde.

The Prince of Wales
Not to of known Oscar Wilde was not to be known.

George Bernard Shaw
He was the greatest conversationalist of his time.
All my work was due to the influence of Oscar Wilde.

Bono of U2
The importance of being Oscar.

The Rolling Stones once made a short movie about Oscar.

Tom Stoppard
He was a hero on humanity.

OSCAR WILDE

CONTENTS

PHOTOGRAPHS AND LANDMARKS

OSCAR WILDE

FOREWORD

Oscar Wilde is arguably the most quoted man in history. He arrived in New York with nothing to declare but his genius in 1882. On his return to England he had London at his feet. In 1895 he was charged and convicted of homosexual activities. He was born in Dublin in October 1854 and died a broken man in exile in Paris on 30th November 1900. He always said his memory would live on.

Importance of being well quoted these quotes cover Wilde's life from when he was a man sitting on his throne to when he went into the gutter.

Full of dazzling wit from his plays, stories, poems, essays and letters. For business and everyday life "nothing succeeds like excess". Quote your genius.

ON HIMSELF

I was a man who stood in symbolic relations to the art and culture of my age. I had realised this for myself at the very dawn of my manhood, and had forced my age to realise it afterwards... Byron was a symbolic figure, but his relations were to the passion of his age and its weariness of passion. Mine were to something more noble, more permanent, of more vital issue, of larger scope. The Gods had given me almost everything, I had genius, a distinguished name, high social position, brilliancy, intellectual daring, I made art a philosophy and philosophy an art: I altered the minds of men and the colours of things: there was nothing I said or did that did not make people wonder: Whatever I touched I made beautiful.

... Now I am completely penniless, and absolutely homeless. Yet there are worse things in the world than that. I am quite candid when I say that rather than go out from this prison with bitterness in my heart against the world, I would gladly and readily beg my bread from door to door. If I got nothing from the house of the rich I would get something at the house of the poor. Those who have much are often greedy; those who have little always share.... 'where I walk there are thorns'.

Oscar Wilde

FACTFILE

1854-1900

1854	Oscar Fingal O'Flahertie Wills Wilde born 16 October in Dublin.
1874	Wilde leaves Trinity College, Dublin and goes up to Magdalen College, Oxford.
	Already his wit and his style of dress have established his reputation as an aesthete.
1881	His first collection of poems published.
	Gilbert and Sullivan's opera PATIENCE satirises Wilde as self-styled leader of the aesthetic movement.
1884	Marries Constance Mary Lloyd, daughter of a well known Irish barrister. She bears him two sons in the next two years. Cyril and Vyvyan.
1888	Publishes THE HAPPY PRINCE.
1890	THE PICTURE OF DORIAN GRAY is published and branded "immoral". W.H. Smith refused to stock this "filthy book".
1892	Meets and falls in love with Lord Alfred Douglas ("Bosie), son of the Marquess of Queensberry (creator of the rules of boxing).
	LADY WINDERMERE'S FAN first performed.
	SALOME banned from production by The Lord Chamberlain.
1893	A WOMEN OF NO IMPORTANCE first performed.

FACTFILE

1895   AN IDEAL HUSBAND opens at the Haymarket and THE IMPORTANCE OF BEING EARNEST at the St. James's Theatre.

Queensberry, denied admission to the first night of IMPORTANCE. Leaves his calling card for Wilde accusing him of being "a somdomite" (sic). Wilde unsuccessfully sues him for libel, and as a result is arrested and tried for homosexuality. After a retrial he is sentenced to two years hard labour. IMPORTANCE AND AN IDEAL HUSBAND are closed.

1897   Writes a letter to BOSIE. Later published as DE PROFUNDIS. Constance is granted custody of the children. Wilde is released from prison and writes the Ballod of Reading Gaol, and leaves England for good.

1900   Wilde is received into the Roman Catholic Church, in Paris on his deathbed.

1900   Oscar Wilde dies a broken man in and is buried in Paris. Lord Alfred Douglas attends the funeral.

1995   To mark the centenary year of The Importance of Being Earnest, a window pane is dedicated to him in Poet's Corner in Westminster Abbey, London.

OSCAR WILDE

THE LORD OF LANGUAGE

Oscar Wilde was one of the most flamboyant literary characters of the last or any other centuries. George Bernard Shaw wrote of Wilde 'He was the finest talker of his time – perhaps of all time. A fitting tribute from one Irish Genius to another. He was born in Dublin in 1854. His father who had been knighted by Queen Victoria, Sir William Wilde a surgeon was one of Dublin's many great characters. A man never drunk but seldom sober, who also liked other women. His mother renowned for her nationalism, was the product of a conservative protestant family, an accomplished talker, and one of the finest hostesses of the day. He was the second of three children having a brother Willie and sister Isola who died when she was nine. When Oscar was born he was a disappointment to his mother, she very much had her heart set on a daughter.

But to make up for his gender mistake, she decided to let Oscar's hair grow into curls and ringlets, until he was nine years old.

Oscar Wilde is probably the most quoted man in history and once said his memory would live on. Even today his wicked wit lives on. His plays, novels and cutting wit had London at his feet. He boasted that he could talk on any subject. A claim proved by the wicked and witty examples in this publication.

Oscar Wilde was educated at Trinity College, Dublin and Magdalen College, Oxford. For fifteen years he enjoyed public acclaim as an author, poet, wit and conversationalist. He consorted with princes and showgirls and was sought after in the most fashionable circles of society for his masterful conversation. He once said he wrote plays to amuse himself.

OSCAR WILDE

Legends sprang up about him and some unsavoury rumours too. He was accused of plagiarism, although he was one of the kindest of men was not widely known. His brilliance as a writer is the sympathy he showed for society's victims. There is no doubt that his language is his finest achievement.

In 1882, upon arriving in New York Customs, Oscar was asked if he had anything to declare and replied in true Wilde fashion, "I have nothing to declare but my genius", which was immediately met with a tumultuous outcry of laughter.

He played everywhere, talking to cowboys, miners and screaming mobs of women. He even told the world that while in America he had to hire two secretaries. One hired to write his autograph and to answer the hundreds of letters that come begging for it and another who's hair was brown to send locks of it to ladies who requested his, he was rapidly becoming bald. He was a riot wherever he went and arrived back in London more famous and even more wanted by the hostesses of the day. There is no doubt that this American tour was definitely the making of Oscar Wilde.

He never suffered fools gladly, but often made sensible men seem foolish, especially when they tried to cross swords with him. At his trial Edward Carson, a fellow undergraduate of Wilde's at Trinity College Dublin, put it to Wilde, "You are of the opinion, I believe that there is no such thing as an immoral book", to which Wilde replied "Yes".

Carson: "May I take it that you think the priest and acolyte was not immoral.

Wilde: "It was worse, it was badly written."

On one occasion when he was called upon to uphold his boast that he could talk spontaneously on any subject a cry went

OSCAR WILDE

up, "The Queen". Without pausing Wilde replied, the queen is not a subject. His wit and humour were so much part of his make-up that he often had audiences enthralled for hours. He knew and met everyone including the Pope and commented, "I was deeply impressed and my walking stick showed signs of budding." He once said that nothing ages like happiness and certainly Oscars aged quickly, before the end of his unique and remarkable career.

It was rumoured around London that he was homosexual, which he sometimes hinted at. Eventually it became the reason he was incarcerated, homosexuality was not a practice accepted in such archaic times as Wilde lived in. Unfortunately Oscar was not made for hard labour in a nineteenth century English prison, particularly a man of his upbringing. On his release he moved to Paris where he died a broken man in exile on November 30th 1900. On his Deathbed he was reported to have said, "I am fighting a duel to the death with the wallpaper, one or the other of us has to go." Some of his so-called friends snubbed Wilde as an ex-convict but entertained him gladly enough in their memoirs. Oscar Wilde was no doubt the greatest comic playwright in the history of literature. Oscar once said his memory would live on, which is why we owe it to Oscar to allow the world to somehow gain insight into the real Oscar Wilde through this publication.

He left a legacy of plays, letters, poetry, criticism, but undoubtedly none more so than his remarkable ability as a wit. I hope you enjoy your one hundred favourites. After all it does show the importance of remembering

Oscar

Lillie Langtry, who Oscar Wilde fell in love with, and who claimed to have helped him in his hour of need and also charmed the Prince of Wales.

I would rather have discovered Lillie Langtry than discovered America.

Library at Trinity College, home to the world famous Book of Kells.

My own business bores me, I prefer other peoples.

THE INTELLECT

*It is only
the intellectually
lost who
never argue.*

(THE PICTURE OF DORIAN GRAY)

I adore simple pleasures, they are the last refuge of the complex.

*All bad art
is the result
of good
intentions.*

(THE PICTURE OF DORIAN GRAY)

We Irish are too poetical to be poets, we are a nation of brilliant failures.

(IN CONVERSATION TO W.B. YEATS, LONDON 1891)

It is a much cleverer thing to talk nonsense than to listen to it.

(AN IDEAL HUSBAND)

I am not English, I am Irish, which is quite another thing.

The Oscar Wilde Autumn School in Bray, Co. Wicklow.

8

The only way to get rid of temptation is to yield to it.

Those who find ugly meanings in beautiful things are corrupt without being charming. This is a fault.

The first duty in life is to be as artificial as possible. What the second is no one has yet discovered.

Friendship is far more tragic than love, it lasts longer. In marriage, three is company and two is one.

To be natural is such a very difficult pose to keep up.

Wilde posing on his American tour

What people call insincerity is simply a method by which we can multiply our personalities.

The condition of perfection is idleness, the aim of perfection is youth.

FROM THE PICTURE OF DORIAN GRAY

Probably the earliest photograph of Oscar Wilde, as you can see, superstition made many mothers dress their boys in girls clothing.

Youth smiles without a reason. It is one of its chiefest charms.

I never put off till tomorrow what I can possibly do the day after.

The soul is born old but grows young. This is the comedy of life, and the body is born young and grows old. that is life's tragedy.

In matters of grave importance, style, not sincerity is the vital thing.

DULLNESS

Wilde age 28.

Only dull people are brilliant at breakfast.

<small>(An Ideal Husband)</small>

I hate vulgar realism in literature. The man who would call a spade a spade should be compelled to use one.

(THE PICTURE OF DORIAN GRAY)

A bad man is the sort of man who admires innocence and a bad woman is the sort of woman a man never gets tired of.

(A WOMAN OF NO IMPORTANCE)

Women have a much better time then men in this world, there are far more things forbidden to them.

PRISON

Interior shot of Reading Gaol where Wilde was incarcerated. His prisoner number was c.33.

Behind my prisons blinded bars, I do possess what none can take away.

I always pass on good advice. It is the only thing to do with it, it is never of any use to oneself.

(AN IDEAL HUSBAND)

We are all in the gutter, but some

Wilde aged 40

of us are looking at the stars.

The public is wonderfully tolerant. It forgives everything except genius.

(THE CRITIC AS ARTIST)

Wilde behind bars – The hypocrisy of Victorian Society.

Families are so mixed nowadays, indeed as a rule, everybody turns out to be somebody else.

(AN IDEAL HUSBAND)

Anyone can sympathise with the sufferings of a friend, but it requires a very fine nature to sympathise with a friend's success.

A GENTLEMAN

It is a very ungentlemanly thing to read a private cigarette case.

(THE IMPORTANCE OF BEING EARNEST)

30

I was deeply impressed and my walking stick showed signs of budding.

(ON MEETING THE POPE)

ON HIS GENIUS

I have nothing to declare except my genius.

(PASSING THROUGH CUSTOMS)

32

*How kind of you
and I shall look
forward to the
royalties.*

(WHEN SOMEONE NAMED A

SILVER MINE AFTER HIM)

Alcohol often drunk in sufficient quantities can sometimes bring on the signs of drunkenness.

To love oneself is the beginning of a lifelong romance.

THE FLORIST

Going into a florist's shop in London, he asked for several bunches of flowers to be removed from the window. With pleasure sir, how many would you like? Asked the assistant.

Oh I don't want any thank you, but they do look rather tired.

I never travel without my diary, one should always have something sensational to read on the train.

Nothing should be out of the reach of hope. Life is a hope.

(A WOMAN OF NO IMPORTANCE)

38

*21 Westland Row
where Wilde was
born.*

The one duty we owe to history is to rewrite it.

(THE CRITIC AS ARTIST)

ON TAXATION

The taxman called to Wilde's door one day about the taxes.

Taxes! Why should I pay taxes.

But sir you live here, you sleep here?

Ah yes, but then you see, I sleep so badly.

I have never given adoration to anybody except myself.

In America the president reigns for four years and journalism governs forever and ever.

(THE SOUL OF MAN UNDER SOCIALISM)

PLEASURE

Wilde looking serious.

Pleasure is the only thing that one should live for.

(AN IDEAL HUSBAND)

All women become like their mothers. That is their tragedy. No man does, that is his.

(A WOMAN OF NO IMPORTANCE)

ON ERROR

Experience is the name everyone gives to their mistakes.

(LADY WINDERMERE'S FAN)

Photo of
Wilde as a
young boy.

Where there is a man who exercises authority, there is a man who resists authority.

(THE SOUL OF MAN UNDER SOCIALISM)

CONTEMPLATION

If I hadn't my debts I shouldn't have anything to think about.

(A WOMAN OF NO IMPORTANCE)

The world is a stage but the play is badly cast.

<small>(LORD ARTHUR SAVILLE'S CRIME)</small>

I am always astonishing myself, it is the only thing that makes life worth living.

The plaque outside No. 1 Merrion Square where Wilde lived from 1855-1878

The well bred contradict other people. The wise contradict themselves.

Always forgive your enemies.

Nothing annoys them so much.

Wilde at twenty.

SCANDAL

I can believe anything provided that it is quite incredible!

(THE PICTURE OF DORIAN GRAY)

Statue of Oscar in coffin at Charring Cross in London

Society produces rogues and education makes one rogue cleverer than another.

To live is the rarest thing in the world. Most people exist that is all.

Statue of Oscar Wilde in Merrion Square, opposite the house where he once lived.

I am hard at work being idle.

Number 1 Merrion Square, where Oscar Wilde lived for many years.

Wisdom is knowing how little we know.

WOMEN

Women are meant to be loved not understood.

(THE SPHINX WITHOUT A SECRET)

To succeed one must have wealth, at all costs one must have wealth.

Where will it all end? Half the world does not believe in God, and the other half does not believe in me.

(TO AMERICAN NOVELIST, MARION CRAWFORD, 1882)

Wilde was once asked to list his favourite 100 books but said that he could not. Why is that? Asked the man who had sought the list. Because I have only written five.

Well my name is Ernest in town and Jack in the country and the cigarette case was given to me in the country.

Good looks are a snare that every man would like to be caught in.

(THE IMPORTANCE OF BEING EARNEST)

THE POET

Trinity College Dublin where Wilde was educated before moving to Oxford.

The Poet is Wilde but his poetry's tame.

Fashion is what one wears oneself, what is unfashionable is what other people wear.

(AN IDEAL HUSBAND)

It is better to have loved and lost, than have never loved at all.

(REFERRING TO FLORENCE BALCOMBE PROBABLY
WILDE'S FIRST LOVE, WHO LATER MARRIED
BRAM STOKER, AUTHOR OF DRACULA)

History never repeats itself. The historians repeat each other. There is a wide difference.

Glass window at Westminster Abbey.

I like to talk to myself. It is one of my greatest pleasures. I often have long conversations all by myself and I am so clever that sometimes I don't understand a single word of what I am saying.

I choose my friends for their good looks my acquaintances for their good character and my enemies for their intellect.

To be spoken of and not to be spoken to is delightful.

THE CRITIC

Wilde on his tour of America in 1882.

Criticism is the highest form of autobiography.

*Young men want
to be faithful
and are not,
old men want to be
faithless and
cannot.*

Work is the curse of the drinking classes.

(IN CONVERSATION TO A FRIEND)

There is no sin except stupidity.

(THE CRITIC AS ARTIST)

Signed photographs of Oscar in the room where he died in Paris.

I am wedded to poverty, but in my case the marriage is not a success; I hate the bride that has been given to me.

(JUNE 1899, PARIS)

The doctor is fighting for a theory, the man is fighting for his life.

THE CYNIC

What is a cynic? A man who knows the price of everything and the value of nothing.

(LADY WINDERMERE'S FAN)

The only difference between the saint and the sinner is that every saint has a past and every sinner has a future.

(A WOMAN OF NO IMPORTANCE)

It isn't easy to be anything nowadays, there is such a lot of beastly competition about.

In the old days men had the rack now they have the press.

(An Ideal Husband)

THE SINNER

Let those who know not what temptation is, let those who have walked as we have done, in the red fire of passion, those who's lives are dull and colourless, in a word let those, if any such there be, who have not loved, cast stones against you.

TEMPTATION

Wilde aged 30.

I can resist everything except temptation.

(LADY WINDERMERE'S FAN)

ON HIS DEATH BED

*My wallpaper and
I are fighting a duel
to the death,
one or the other of us
has to go.*

JUDGEMENT

A man cannot be too careful in his choice of enemies.

We women adore failures, they lean on us.

In this world there are two tragedies, one is not getting what one wants and the other is getting it.

(LADY WINDEREMERE'S FAN)

THE YOUNG

The old believe everything, the middle aged suspect everything, the young know everything.

(PHRASES, PHILOSOPHIES FOR THE USE OF THE YOUNG)

The one charm of marriage is that it makes a life of deception absolutely necessary.

The book of life begins with a man and woman in a garden. It ends with revelations.

There is hardly a single person in the house of Commons worth painting, though many of them would be the better for a little whitewashing.

One should either be a work of Art, or wear a work of Art.

(PHRASES, PHILOSOPHIES FOR
THE USE OF THE YOUNG)

There is more brass than brains in the Aristocracy.

(Vera or the Nihilists)

Youth is the Lord of life, youth has a kingdom waiting for it. Everyone is born a king and most people die in exile, like most kings.

(A WOMAN OF NO IMPORTANCE)

There is only one thing in the world worse than being talked about and that is not being talked about.

(THE PICTURE OF DORIAN GRAY)

THE BALLAD OF READING GAOL

Yet each man kills the thing he
loves, by each let this be heard,
Some do it with a bitter look,
Some with a flattering word,
The coward does it with a kiss,
The brave man with a sword!

TALENT AND GENIUS

I have put only my talent into my works, I have put all my genius into my life.

(IN CONVERSATION IN ALGIERS, JANUARY 1885)

SOCIETY

Never speak disrespectfully of society, only people who can't get into it do that.

(THE IMPORTANCE OF BEING EARNEST)

All trials are trials for one's life and all sentences are sentences of death.

(WRITTEN IN PRISON THE
GREATEST SORROW OF WILDE'S LIFE)

One can survive everything nowadays, except death.

Painting of Oscar in the bedroom in the L'Hotel at St. Germain in Paris, where he died.

Oscar Wilde died in disgrace in Paris on 30th November 1900. He is buried in Pere la Chaise Cemetery, Paris.

I shall die as I lived - beyond my means.

To the doctor in Paris, on his death bed on receipt of his medical bill.

I shall never make a new friend in my life, though perhaps a few after I die.